Selected Poems
1965-1995

Jane's copy

Michael

Other Books by Michael Dennis Browne:

The Wife of Winter (Rapp & Whiting, London, 1970)
The Wife of Winter (Charles Scribner, New York, 1970)
Sun Exercises (Red Studio Press, Loretto, MN, 1976)
The Sun Fetcher (Carnegie Mellon, Pittsburgh, 1978)
Smoke from the Fires (Carnegie Mellon, Pittsburgh 1985)
You Won't Remember This (Carnegie Mellon,
                                    Pittsburgh, 1992)

Selected Poems
1965-1995

Michael Dennis Browne

Carnegie Mellon University Press • Pittsburgh • 1997

Acknowledgments

I am grateful to the editors of the following magazines and anthologies in which some of these poems first appeared: *Agassiz Review, American Poetry Review, Aspen Anthology, Black Box, Crazyhorse, Dacotah Territory, Ironwood, One, Prairie Schooner, Seneca Review, Silo, Studio One, The Nation, The Greenfield Review, The Iowa Review, The New Yorker, Tri-Quarterly.*

The New Yorker Book of Poems (Viking); *The Decade Dance* (Sandhills Press); *Best Poems of 1974* (Pacific Books); *Minnesota Writes: Poetry* (Milkweed Editions/Nodin Press); *After the Storm* (Maisonneuve Press); *The American Poetry Anthology* (Avon); *The Sensuous President* (New Rivers Press); *Twenty-Five Minnesota Poets* (Nodin Press); *Best Poems of 1967* (Pacific Books); *This Sporting Life* (Milkweed Editions); *News of the Universe* (Sierra Club Books); *A Tumult for John Berryman* (Dryad Press); *Men of Our Time* (University of Georgia Press); *The Best of Crazyhorse* (University of Arkansas Press); *Brother Songs* (Holy Cow! Press); *The Pushcart Prize III* (The Pushcart Press); *The Rag and Bone Shop of the Heart* (HarperCollins); *The Carnegie Mellon Anthology of Poetry* (Carnegie Mellon); *Life on the Line* (Negative Capability Press); *A Good Man: Fathers and Sons in Poetry and Prose* (Fawcett Columbine); *A Year in Poetry* (Crown); *Drive, They Said* (Milkweed Editions).

Special thanks to Lisa McLean, Chester Anderson, Christine Sikorski, David Bengtson, Jim Moore, and Louis Jenkins. I am very grateful to Gerald Costanzo for his ongoing support.

The publication of this book is supported by a grant from the Pennsylvania Council on the Arts.

Library Congress Catalog Card Number 96-83421
ISBN 0-88748-243-0
ISBN 0-88748-244-9 Pbk.

Contents

Contents, *cont.*

for my family

THE WIFE OF WINTER
1970

PETER

Peter sleep-walks.
And is my brother.

Not knows why. But does.
Not knows why. But is.

Because my father and my mother.

And this night in pajamas
Barefoot
Left the house and walked
Five hundred yards to my sister's house
And knocked
To be let in.

Let me in. I knock.
Let me in.

And walked back,
Saying he did not remember.

I knock. Let me in.
I am asleep.

He was.

O let us in.
We are all asleep.
We are asleep, let us in.

THE VISITOR
for Alex and Hanna Quaade

A fine rain falls, greening their garden.
The ladder into the apple tree drips beads of silk.
Silk rolls from the roof.

They do not play at owning.
The house holds firm in the earth,
the foundations are good,
the earth is black and gripping.

Silk rolls from the roof.

The baby is an electric piece in their hands,
is a portion of their own exactness,
is an ease of them,
passes between them like a blueness.

A fine Danish rain falls.
On a darkened wet August afternoon
that has simply given up.

Red books on their shelves, and purple.
The clock in the hall
springs into the pool of its sound.

To note them is an envy.
This cannot be earned.
It comes to the hands like a cloth. It is given.

What may it be then, and what shall I take
with me tomorrow on the flight to London?
The idea of your marriage in my case?
Like a piece of wood Alex has found and painted?
Do I borrow this Danish idea?

What they have is very difficult.
Not a harbor.
Not silk. It will not swallow.

Greened is the garden, silked by the rain.
The ladder drips like a silver engine.
The apples are hard but glamorous.

I would take a scissors to my own clouds if I could,
weary of playing a Falstaff on quick visits.
I am a thin thin man.

No peace like the peace of this darkened house
in the Danish afternoon.
Christian has one tooth and sleeps.
Alex has a red book with his own poems
            written in it.
Hanna cooks and has a hundred real skills.

A fine rain falls,
greened is their garden.

HANDICAPPED CHILDREN SWIMMING
for Lamar

A measure of freedom. Mike, floating,
would not manage so without
the red life-jacket but would sink,

messy as weed; but with it
lies, weak, like a shirt,
and the eyes, and the tongue

uncontrolled, extended, show
the delight it is to be
horizontal on water, strapped there

by nothing but sunlight. Connie,
who otherwise moves with crutches
and stiff braces, is strong

through water. Becky, seeing always
badly, lies washed by the sense
of her own fragility, liking

the help of warm hands. Gregg
rides and plucks at the water
while Danny makes his own music

in his mind as he lilts
completely quiet. Mike's delight
opens like a flower as he floats.

He doesn't know he is floating
now in this poem. I have
nothing in fact to sustain him

and I know he will never stand
up alone. But whatever sustains
the children here is important;

inflamed with the success
of water, released, they mingle
and soften there, as wax

on wetness, limp as wet bread
on water's kindness. Those fingers
can grasp as competently at air

and water as mine. Their bodies
are milky and do not need
cleansing, except from deformity.

Water cannot wash their
awkwardness from them, water is
simple, and their defects difficult;

but they ride for a while, never
as free as the times they fly
in dreams, over the cliffs

harvesting in the sea, the bats
exquisite with radar, but
something, a measure of freedom.
And Mike is lucid on water,

still physically cryptic, physically
glinting, but Mike has grace

for a while, this is his best
floating since before birth,
where he lay bunched like any

other unformed — encircled, contained,
his mother not knowing the
uncontrol of those limbs that

threshed and kicked at her
from out of that orchard of water,
Light strolls among them, padding

healthy, firm, as these imperfect
children perch rolling in the foliage
of water, shifting to new flowerings

of face, though their limbs are
weeds. The shock comes when you see
the muscular men who played

with them in the pool carry them
in huddles from the pool, sunlight
spreading its crime on them.

THE DELTA

There are men making death together in the wood

We have not deserved this undergrowth
We have not merited this mud
O Jesus this mud

There are men making death together in the wood

My sergeant lies in a poisoned shadow
My friend has choked on a flower
The birds are incontinent in their terror

There are men making death together in the wood

They have taken my hands away
And they have hidden me from the moon
Pain makes decisions all around me

There are men making death together in the wood

The fish are puzzled among darkening knots
        of water
The ancient stairways of light sway and spill
The ferns are stained with the yellow blood
        of stones

There are men making death together in the wood

We have hidden the children for safety
      beneath the water
And the children are crying to us
      through the roots of the trees
They are soft pebbles without number
And they fill the streams

And the moon appears to watch now white with
grief

See them now
Pilgrimming unwilling into dying
Unburdened now of blood
Their hurt bodies soaked with the dusk
See the reluctant file

In a line he leads them
In a long slow line

They leave us over the hill
They are grass
They are dust
They are shed stone
Cold as the moon

And the widow moon above
Is cold and white
And will let no lovers in tonight

ELEGY

for Kate Houskeeper and Elie Siegel, students of Bennington College, who died in an automobile accident, April 7, 1969

Birds on the branch outside my window.
I wish they were Elie,
I wish they were Kate.

I wish they were taking a shower
or going to lunch. I wish Elie was
making more music, notes of her own,
lovely, serious and slim, expertly
on the violin. I wish Kate was
arranging her curls. Kate, I will miss
your curls, where you sat, in the front
of the class, listening.
But the girls have gone into the dark.

I wish you were vain,
I wish you had time to touch yourselves,
in front of mirrors,
in front of lovers.

I want Elie just once more
to lay her hands on Mozart,
to play as I saw her play,
intent, at just one concert.
I do not want you thrown
out of a car, your lives,
an evening in April, when I was driving
the same way, back, back here.

But I arrived. And am alive.
I stopped once to watch
the last of light over the hills.
Maybe you went by me then;
for sure you went by me for ever.

The day of your death I fell asleep
in the afternoon; and woke, afraid,
dreaming I had run down
the dark ladders of afternoon,
down, always down; and was glad to find
no wife lay at my side, to share
in my fear.

                    But you further
and faster than I, life saying
these I do not want, these
I do not choose to have, to learn, to make
more music, to love, I do not want
these hands poring over my face,
I will cast them forever.

And today, the Spring lake
bright like blue ploughland, a warmer
wind through the trees,
the evergreens rocking and dipping their limbs
and even the rocks putting out little hands inside,
here are we who must make
music for you now,
from the cello, the shining violin,
lament for the makers, for the makers are gone,
but the music goes on.

But for you,
all making, all music, all love,
lying down for ever
with the earth that is newer by far
than ever before.

And birds on the branch beside my window,
singing too soon, singing too late;
in April, birds with their clear new song.
I wish they were Elie. I wish they were Kate.

THE SUN FETCHER
1978

EPITHALAMION/WEDDING DAWN
for Nicholas & Elena

1

Happy the man who is thirsty.
And the moths, pilgrims to our screens.
The fisher stands waist-deep in the water,
waiting. Happy the man waiting.

Who is not alone? Who does not sleep
in the dark house of himself, without music?
The world, a collapsed fire, shows only its smoke,
and the smoke hides its hills,

hides, too, the places where we are sleeping,
the hand opened, the hand closed.
Fragments, the lovers lie. And the question,
saying:

Who is broken? No one is broken,
but the living are sleeping, like animals,
like the dead. Tree dreams
of the man he was, who walked

by the shore, who followed
the hill upward, who dragged his roots
through the universe, who lay down
to suffer there, and, loving the earth,

left it exhausted, returned to it renewed.
But the house is dark. The sky at such time
has no light. Even the lines in the hand
are a little desert without name, and silent.

2

Friends; in the hours before dawn;
the day of your wedding.
What will I tell you then?
That solitude's thorn
breaks into bloom now? I think it is so.
I think that if we are scarred, light heals us now.
We can be heard, making our difficult music.
And for this the sun
drags itself up from the dark parts of the world,
again, again.
The windows take on the peculiar fire of the living.
The dog hoots like a wood-pigeon, he has
his morning.

3

You must not be angry with this planet.
For we are in a company
whose music surpasses its pain.
For I tell you, I sat in the dark, also,
and the wedding light came onto my window,
and the hills were cleared for me,
and the field spread out in front of me,
remarkable, like marble.
And I thought: this is their day,
how it breaks for them!

O sir, the angel flies, even with bruises.
O lady, a bird can wash himself anywhere.
The dawn that came up the day of your wedding
took me in its hand like the creature I am;
and I heard the dark that I came from
whispering "Be silent."
And the dawn said "Sing."
And I found the best words I could find around me,
and came to your wedding.

HALLOWE'EN 1971

I carve my first head. Then I carve another.
Now I have two Vietnamese
children on my table.

I place a candle in each of them, & light it.
The heads are still wet inside. I've put
the seeds in a brown bag.

I take one head to the window.
The other I put on my stair, with the front
door open. By it, a bowl of candy.

2

Down the block,
round the neighborhood,
all over this darkened country,
the hollow yellow heads
burning in windows, & tiny
American ghosts running toward them
through the dark, with open hands.

OWL
    to John Berryman

On November 30th, 1972, a Great Horned Owl was seen high in a
tree on the University of Minnesota campus, between Walter Library
and Johnston Hall. The owl stayed there all day; by the following
morning he was gone.

He is there, with his large eyes,
high above us,
who were never close.
He will not say, he will not say
what it is he wants.
But we are glad he is there,
we without wings.
There is nothing he need not do.
And if he jumps,
we need not fear for him.

WAYS OF LOOKING AT SNOW DOG
for Keith Gunderson

1

In sleep, there is nothing I cannot do
& I love my extraordinary life.

But in the sun through the window
I see the human hand lift into light,

& my dog's dish is empty.
And I rise, as all the world rises,

going for water.

2

He sighs.
When I am making
a point about poetry in class,
he lets out
such a sigh, *I've heard it
all before, dear
but repetitive master.*

When I am reading out loud
& reach a part of a poem
I care about,
he will rise, & start
to chase his tail,
I lose my listeners.

He climbs all over my students.
He will chase anything
to lick it.
There is just about nothing
he will not kiss.
Especially small children;
he sprints after them
while the mothers stand
paralyzed;
and he slobbers all over them.

3

you are the magic dog, at night a lost sailor looks
        out of your eyes
you are the magic dog, so white, when I take you
        skiing they say, *see, he talks to himself*
you are the magic dog, you chase squirrels,
        you will never make it
you are the magic dog, at night you float,
        you bear the children on your back
you are the magic dog, you growl in the house,
        you bark at the footfall
you are the magic dog, when I get sad & sunk
        in my life, there is your life
        in front of me, shaming my sadness
you are the magic dog, at the parking lot
        the attendant sees you in the back & asks
        if I will park the car myself,
        I explain your kindness
you are the magic dog, you peed on the office
        Christmas tree, well, you must think,

inside or out, tree is a tree
is a tree is a tree

4

Sometimes I think he is wise.
He is a guide, a little mythical.

Sometimes he gives me long looks,
he has grave eyes.

Sometimes he has the face of my father.
But when I call him, he comes,
as the dead man does not.

Sometimes when he lies half-sleeping on the floor
I say his name, or praise him,
& his tail breaks the silence,
thump, thump, thump.

Sometimes he lays his jaw on my shoe
& I feel far below us
another pair is there,
the skull of a head
on the skull of a foot, resting.

5

The stick! The stick!
You want the stick,
any stick will do,
the stick is sweet to you!

It flies through the air
like a bone filled with fuel,
you wrench it off the earth
& bring it right back.

But you don't *give* it back.
You run circles around me, the best game.
All over the planet, in parks,
breathless men pleading with their dogs

for the magic wand in their jaws.

6

In the dark wind I run with my dog.
He is so white, he is like snow,
& I call him so.
I take the garbage out in brown bags
& I put a match to it.
The flames jump up,
the flames of human rubbish
light up his eyes.

7

At night I lie
stretched out, still.
I am the knight on the tomb, marble,
and you are the hound
carved forever at my feet.
But we breathe.

8

At the clinic he goes in
the entrance for SMALL ANIMALS.
A small horse. Eighty pounds.
They run a test on his eyes
& the rims go green.
Then the green runs out of his nose.
He sits, wretched
on the metal table
with his white-and-green clown face.
His eyes are fine.
For years he can go on running
ahead, taking me deeper.

9

At the zoo too he is small.
When I feel he's getting superior,
bigger than most
dogs on the block,

I take him to the lion, the Bengal tiger.
He can't quite believe what he sees.
He shrinks back:
why have you brought me here?

The white she-wolf, when she sees him.
moans & whines,
she wants to be with him.
But the cougars in the next cage

tear up & down, they fly against the bars,
they want to rip him apart.
I take him off, to chase a safe stick in the park.
There are enough claws around us.

10

He sheds.
I have never seen anything like it.
He carefully chooses
the place to shake himself,
a rug just swept,
a floor just cleaned.
He walks about the house
spraying his white hairs.
When he sleeps on my bed
I wake up old.

11

He likes best to chew
the human hand.
For him it's a kind, inexhaustible object,
a sort of soft sculpture he can get his teeth into.

When I feel
such life on the end of my hand,
tugging me out of my dark,
he seems to be saying —

O man too used to the moon,
leave your dark farm
where the tears fall thick,
I'll lick them off with my tongue.

He seems to crow —

Cock-a-doodle-beginning,
cock-a-doodle-beginning,
rise, rise,
leave your bad bed.

Each stick thrown
is one move forward.
Each walk undertaken
is one shadow not stayed in.

12

I saw the dog's dream

he smelled the summer on the window
he danced with stiff hips

I saw the dog's dream

in the storm he dreamed of his son
the dog wrapped a harp in a blanket

I saw the dog's dream

he sucked a light-bulb as it burned
he ran to the pool where the neighborhood dogs
     swam weeping

I saw the dog's dream

the bone came down in the form of a cloud
the white boat slipped from her mooring

two by two the white dogs go
over the glass harbor

13

you are the magic dog, sweet hound, we will not
     meet in Heaven
you are the magic dog, utterly useless
     as a telephone answering service
you are the magic dog, when the car radio played
     "Jingle Bells" performed by a chorus
     of singing dogs, you nearly
     fell off the seat

you are the magic dog, when you eat your red meat
     I am far from you
you are the magic dog, when your nose is deep
     in another dog, you hardly hear me
you are the magic dog, I will never own you
you are the magic dog, you will never see Denmark
you are the magic dog, your white bark flies up
     to be the moon

you are the magic dog, you sing to the prisoners
you are the magic dog, you scratch at the screen
you are the magic dog, & you want to come in

well, well, come in then, welcome

FOX

Driving fast down the country roads.
To a committee. A class.
When I stop for gas, a highway patrolman tells me
one of my lights is out.
Then he drives off to take up his position
behind a bush at the bottom of the hill
to wait for speeders.

Yesterday, a snake, black & green, coiled
down by the railroad tracks.
His mouth bloody, he moved slowly,
he looked like he was dying.
Boats being pulled up out of the water.
The dog ran into the lake
after the sticks the children threw,
and stood looking back at me from the gold water.

On TV, the faces of the captured Israeli pilots.
Syrian film of Israeli planes crashing,
martial music. The patrolman
crouched behind the bush,
the mouth of the snake, hard & red,
his green-black body without ease,
a bent stick by him, as if maybe
a child had beaten him with it, maybe the same
child throwing sticks to the dog in the water.

Hurrying through Wisconsin.
Hundreds of black birds tossed up
from a cornfield, turning away. Arab or Israeli?
The man in the parked patrol car,
the sticks rushing, failing through the air
County Road Q, County Road E.
The committee meeting, waiting for me.

The fox! It is a fox! It is a red fox!
I slow up. He is in the road.
I slow. He moves into the grass, but not far.
He doesn't seem that afraid.
Look, look! I say to the white dog behind me.
Look, Snow Dog, a fox! He doesn't see him.
And this fox. What he does now is
go a little further, & turn, & look at me.
I am braked, with the engine running,
looking at him.

I say to him, Fox — you Israeli or Arab?
You are red; whose color is that?
Was it you brought blood
to the mouth of the snake? The patrolman
is waiting, the dog standing
in the gold water. Would you
run fetch, what would you
say to my students? He looks at me.

And I say, So go off, leave us, over
the edge of that hill, where we shan't see you.

Go on — as the white she-wolf can't,
who goes up & down, up & down
against her bars all day,
all night maybe.

Be fox for all of us, those in zoos,
in classrooms, those on committees,
neither Assistant Fox nor Associate Fox
but Full Fox, fox with tenure, runner
on any land, owner of nothing, anywhere,
fox beyond all farmers,
fox neither Israeli nor Arab,
fox the color of the fall & the hill.

And you, O fellow with my face,
do this for me: one day
come back to me, to my door,
show me my own crueller face, my face
as it really cruelly is, beyond what
a committee brings out in me, or the woman
I love when I have to leave her.
But no human hand, fox untouched, fox
among the apples & barns, O call out
in your own fox-voice through the air
over Wisconsin that is full
of the falling Arab & Israeli leaves,
red, red, locked together, falling
in spirals, burning . . .

Be a realler, cleaner thing,
no snake with a broken body, no bent stick,
no patrolman crouched behind a bush
with bloody mouth, no stick thrown,
no beloved tamed dog in the water . . .

And let us pull up now out of the water
the boats, & call the leaves home
down out of the air, Arab or Israeli;
& you, my real red fox in Wisconsin,
as I let out the clutch & leave you,
you come back that time, be cruel then,
teach me your fox-stink even, more than now, as I
hurry, kind & fragrant, into committee,
& the leaves falling, red, red.
And the fox runs on.

ROBERT BLY GETS UP EARLY

At the ticket counter, Minneapolis Airport, 7:30 am, standing in line — a hand on my shoulder! It is Robert Bly! Risen like a silo from out of the dark earth for one last greeting.

He is flying to Boston to read. Flying to Boston with a satchel of red bees. "I have red bees in my bag. I will have no hesitation in releasing them into your unconscious."

Robert Bly! Organic Foods! White Poncho! Vitamin E!

I get on my plane, sit down with *Esquire*, *The New Yorker*, and *Greek Lyric Poetry*. I reach for my notebook to write down a few bad lines about Robert Bly unexpectedly putting his hand on my shoulder so early in the morning at the airport — when a man sits down beside me — it is Robert Bly!

This plane goes to Pittsburgh but he has charmed his way harshly past the stewardesses. He flies simultaneously to so many places in his head, why should he not think that the Pittsburgh plane will take him also to his reading in Boston — perhaps even directly to the podium!

What does this manic Son of Norway want of me?
He shoves a small blue book into my hands. It is
by a young Norwegian poet who is traveling around
the country in a Greyhound Bus with his girlfriend.

Do we have money for him, he asks? His eyes
crackle with the lustre of Vitamin E.

O Robert Bly, you are on this earth only briefly, like
an angel with a hangover. I see you striding, wings
folded, across the main lobby of the Minneapolis
International Airport, pushing a vast plow. From the
shattered floor foams a tide of soldier ants, Latvian
attorneys, centurions, phantoms, admirals, minor
poets with half-opened parachutes. They flow out of
the airport and into the landscape, determined to
turn the country around.

O Robert Bly, get off my plane! I have two readings
of my own to do in Pittsburgh!

Robert Bly hurtles to gate 7a with his satchel of bees.
He gets on his plane — at last! He needs no charm now —
he has a ticket! From deep in the poncho he releases
a bee. The bee makes his way forward into the cabin,
crawls up onto the pilot's shoulder, and croaks into
his ear: "Take this plane to 4th-century Tibet."

MY FATHER'S MUSIC

For fourteen years I have not heard
that Bach prelude played for me as I sat
alone in the back of the church.
Fourteen years since my dear musician died.

And she plays my father's music now,
this woman in Minnesota.
Not his, I know now,
but the sounds he served
in the dark church. My childhood.

I thought I could write of
myself as the son rising
finally from the father, that I could be
as a rose over his grave, rooted but
staying bloomed, there at my zenith.

But now I know I must often go down, fold
over into him, & others play that music,
& weep, as today I did, hearing her,
that if I rise — and I *feel* risen — I must
go down again, & again rise,

my days a falling, a rising again,
those chords keeping me company,
those hands clustering to press & loose the music,
those forests sons walk in, seeking the father,
themselves the father, & seeking the son.

BIRD BEFORE DAWN

Bird before dawn,
bird before dawn,
I hear you

liquid in the dark,
long before
the light,

hear you
after hours of images,
tethered

to the Great Silence,
eyes closed, lips open
but no music from me;

and now though I lie
a human in a room,
I am there

in your throat,
in the wet center
where the notes swell,

without words,
with merely a man's tongue;
and O my musician,

my April chanter,
I rise, I ride
out of the winter on your song.

TALK TO ME, BABY

1

A friend at a cocktail party tells me
of being on a fishing trip up North
and meeting some men from Illinois
who showed him how to clean and filet
a fish properly; and of how, when one
particular pike was stripped
almost clean, almost all of him gone,
the jaw with the razory teeth opened
and some kind of cry came from the creature,
that head on the end of almost no body;
and the man with the knife said:
"Talk to me, baby."

2

Up in the Boundary Waters last weekend
I hooked a trout, my first, and played him.
I got him to the shallows and tried
to raise him. And we got down
into the water with my leather hat —
we hadn't brought a net — and I was yelling
"I've got a fish! I've got a fish!"
out into the evening, and we tried
to get him into the hat, and did once,
but then he was out again — a wriggle, a flap —
that fish jumped out of my hat! —
and the line, gone loose, jerked, snapped,

and he was back in the water,
the hook in him.

And he didn't turn into
a glimmering girl, like he did for
young Willie Yeats, nor was he
a Jesus, like for Lawrence; he just
drifted head down near the shallows,
huge, the huge hook in him.
And Louis and Phil came up in the other
canoe, and we got the flashlight on him,
and tried to get hold of him. But then, somehow,
we lost him, drifting about, he was not there
but gone somewhere deeper into the water,
every minute darker; my hook in him.

I hooked five or six snags after that, yelling
each time that each one was a fish, bigger
than the last. But I brought nothing living up.
And the other canoe went silvery on the water,
and the pines were massed, dark, and stood
and smelled strong, like a bodyguard
of dried fish.

3

Breathing, my brother in my house,
and breathing, his wife beside him.

Breathing, my brother in America,
his body in my bed, her body.

Their tent the color of the sun in my garden.

And they are riding West.

And both of us riding West, brother,
since we swam out of the father,

heading, six years apart,
the same way.

The dog stares at me, not knowing
why I have not fed him.
The cat crying to come in.

Whom we feed, sustain us.
Who need us, we keep breathing for.

I have seen you, at supper with friends,
put your hands to the guitar strings

and bring strong music out, seen you
sit and pick out

a tune on the piano,
on a friend's penny whistle.

To hold an instrument, to play.
To hold a pen, to write.

To do as little harm as possible
in the universe, to help

all traveling people, West, West;
you are not traveling alone,

not ever; we all go with you;
only the body stays behind.

4

When I stand on my island, a Napoleon,
one hand nailed to my chest,
the writing hand;

when I can only *stare*
at the ocean, at the birds
running and turning against the light . . .

when I am
the Illinois man and his kind,
"Talk to me, baby,"

the one with the knife inside, sometimes,
the one you may meet on your travels,
the one behind you in the line to get on the bus,

the one arranging a deal in a phone booth
as you drive past,
when I become that thing I sometimes become,

I will go into
the green of this visit, the green
you asked me to try to see

after my earlier, darker poems for you —
and this, the fourth one, darker
than I meant, since the man with the knife

swam into it — O when that killer
stands over our city, our sleeping and loving places,
tent, canoe, cabin of sweet people —

I will hear with your ears
the songs of the birds of the new world
that so quicken you, and look for

their wings that flame and flash — there! there!
among the leaves and branches . . .

5

Too often I have wanted
to slip away, the hook in me,
to roll off the bed
and into the dark waters under it:
to drift, head down,
hide, hide, the hook in me;
to roll
in the wet ashes of the father,
wet with the death of the father,
and not try
to burn my way upward; the son, rising.

I swear to you now, I will survive,
rise up, and chant my way through these losses.

And you, you, brother, whatever that is,
same blood, you who swim
in the same waters,
you promise me to make *your* music too,
whatever the hurt;

O when we are almost only
mouth, when we are almost only a head
stuck on the pole of the body,
and the man says "Talk to me, baby,"
let's refuse him, brother, both, all of us,
and striking the spine like an instrument, inside,
like birds, with even the body broken,
our feathers fiery — there! there! — among
the leaves and branches, make
no sounds he will know;
like birds, my brother, birds of the new world, *sing*.

SUN EXERCISES

One: Face the Sun. Fold the hands. Legs together. Stand erect.

I am walking by the sea with my mother.

There is a jail built on the sand,
at the water's edge.
We hear faint cries from inside,
the jail rocks softly,
like a box with an animal inside it

In a small boat my father goes by.
It is a calm sea.
Rowing with him are his father
and his father's father.
As the three men go by,
my father pauses from his rowing
and waves to us.
My sister Mary is standing on the beach.
She is staring into the sun.
Her belly swells, she must lie down.
I ask her why she lies down on the sand;
she says:
"To give birth to my pain."
After a little while, her belly subsides,
 she lies quiet.

My sister Angela stands looking at the waves;
like a Queen she tries to command them:
"Go back, go back." The tide creeps forward,
licks at her feet.
Her hands are resting on a pram;
the pram is filled with fish, small fish,
of a kind you can catch in any country.

The tide comes in; she steps back,
letting the pram go:
it floats off from her.
How soon do we turn to men,
who swim in the sea?

And here is my mother, content to sit
and watch the water.
She is remembering when she was a girl,
and the long long wrinkled hair of the four sisters.
She is content to be dreaming of them
in the long afternoon.

My three women of the sand.

Peter comes up to me.
Evening already. A darker blue.
He has coils of ropes on both shoulders.
My brother is Prince of Ropes.
He says: "It's time to go."
My brother at home among heights,
which I fear.
He says: "We must rope up."

Soon we are bound together.
We walk to the base of the steep cliff.
It goes up and up,
I cannot see the top.
Evening already. A night coming down.
We make the first toe-holds,
we begin to climb
the high stone face of the father.

Two: Inhale and raise the arms. Bend backward.

You, I accuse.
You, Michael Moon.

Mad Moon Boy.
How mad you are, nobody knows.

You get drunk at dawn.
You ride the spider bareback across the dawn.

You stand on your head on the moon,
alone. Little Tomb Lover.
Ophelia, Ophelia, drifting along;
ah, such a sad song!

When you were small,
what was your nightmare?
My nightmare was
that the moon rose over the world's edge;
it stared at me; it climbed, it smiled,
and was mocking me.

If I didn't wake myself up
before it climbed too high.
I'd be dead.

What now do you dream?
I feel the shadows of Europe creep
over my sheets.
I hear the French,
I hear Agincourt and its arrows.

I see my brain,
my brain the potato,
the black three-pound potato
in an Irish field.
I hold up my brain,
caked with the dirt of ancestors,
I wave it —
do all my thoughts
come from this thing?

I rinse it in a stream
like an old washerwoman,
I race through the streets,
this moon-brain in my hands.

Eli, Eli, lama sabachtani? *
This is the night the dead headmaster
turns toward you with a fresh exam,
this is the night the crucifix clicks open
under the black gloves of the burglar.

This is the night the rat runs out
for his free gift,
this is the night
the boneless bird
flies.

This is the night the children
crouch in the stone rocket,
this is the night a mother chains
her child to a dead animal.

Eddie, Eddie . . .

O you Moon,
you Potato Man,
you Toy —
how can we rid the town of this rat?

Moon, I summon you.
Michael Moon, I call you out
from your shallow grave,

from your brown bag
in the Potter's Field — come forth.
"Moon get up and mend your wounds —"
all the children know *that* song.

See, the rocking chair rocks backwards and forwards,
trying to rock itself into a man —
"Moon get up and mend your wounds —"
See, the woman croons a quiet song
to the driftwood she holds in her arms.

Moon,
Michael Moon,
mend yourself,
come forth.

My God, my God, why hast Thou forsaken me?

*Three: Exhale and bend forward till the hands are in line
with the feet. Touch the knees with your head.*

Easter again.
I light a candle in the window.

On a hill in Wisconsin
I light a hundred candles;
O little prisoners,
strapped to your wicks, but dancing!

I gather dry wood from behind the house.
I pile and light it.

And I remember the Vigils, Easter Eve,
the night of the new fire;
the whole church darkened,
the priest breathing on the water of the font,
the priest taking
the huge hunk of Paschal candle
and sliding it into the water.

And the kindling of the new fire,
the passing from taper to taper
until all God's people stood
in a flickering, a silence;
each fist flowers with the new fire.

We boys went round with poles,
lifting the Lent cloths off the statues.

Now the sun sinks, into the bluffs
behind the lake.
I say to the sun: "Do you die too?"
He tells me: "No, I go down
to meet the snake, alone.
Always I return."

I rub sticks together,
I dance.
I ride the roads.
I run up and down
the hills on fire,
the peasants of Europe are marching with torches,
run run over Wisconsin now with torches,
through the abandoned farms,
roll blazing wheels down hills,
let there be
beacons on each height,
hoist fires like children
on their fathers' shoulders.

I am the Boy of New Fire.
I am the King you feast from.

I am the Fellow of Flares.
I slide down to the lake — still frozen —
I breathe my English breath three times
on this midwestern water,
and in the pool I make I dip
the moon-corpse, white as the cold
Christ-body of the father,
I the Moon Man
Easter upon myself.

There is my house on the hill, and all its lights
If I could cut a cloth of such flame,
and all winter wear it,
if I could bless and multiply,
if I could pass out
these flames among my friends,
and every house,
like my castle of many candles,
and every family, and friend,
this night receive new fire.

SMOKE FROM THE FIRES
1985

HIDE AND GO SEEK
for Lisa

I count to fifty.
Then I appear at the French window;
in my hand, the three-flame candelabrum.
The children have run to hide in my sister's garden.
It is March, damp dark, that English dark I left.

I make the monster sound.
I give the groan they long to hear, and fear.
I can almost feel their shivering out there.

Then I begin to move.
I lurch, stiff-legged. I sway.
I am the Mud Man, come
still smeared from his swamp,
I am something extinct
with my rotting fingers,
I am the slimy thing from the sea
who leaks after them on feet
horribly like the human hand, but heavier.
I am he no longer afraid of fire,
who points these prongs of flame to find them.
I need some blood.
I need to catch me some family flesh
and chew it down to the bone.

Appalled, they hurtle all over,
the nephews, the nieces,
they scatter, they stream

round Fran and Angela's garden,
desperate scared, mad scared —
who let this thing loose in England? —
run! run! —
the Bogey Man, the Bog Beast —
run! run!

Roaring, reaching out,
again and again I miss them,
so slow I am,
so sleepy with my swampy blood,
miss them just enough to freshen their fear,
to send them screaming further
into the dark,
out behind the beanpoles,
behind the compost,
behind the favorite tree that is now
metal to the touch.
I hear, I hear the panting.

And — it is enough. Now it is done.
Now I raise the candles to show
my friendlier face — I am Michael again,
the almost American uncle,
and I call to them: *All in, All in.*
Together we go toward the house,
through the garden that is theirs again,
laughing, still thrilled with our fright.
And Damien, my godson, four,
that boy of light I sought in the dark,
shouts: "I'm bigger than myself!"

Whoever the seekers, children,
whoever will chase you,
if inside you, if behind you,
may they miss, I pray it,
may they not touch,
may you make it
past such grasping and reach the house
as now together we do,
where people are waiting who love us
and from darkness welcome us.
O mystery of family. O darkness. O house.
I pray it: *All in. All in.*

LAMB

Saw a lamb being born.
Saw the shepherd chase and grab a big ewe
and dump her on her side.
Saw him rub some stuff from a bottle on his hands.
Saw him bend and reach in.
Heard two cries from the ewe.
Two sharp quick cries. Like high grunts.
Saw him pull out a slack white package.
Saw him lay it out on the ground.
Saw him kneel and take his teeth to the cord.
Saw him slap the package around.
Saw it not move.
Saw him bend and put his mouth to it and blow.
Doing this calmly, half kneeling.
Saw him slap it around some more.
Saw my mother watching this.
Saw Angela. Saw Peter.
Saw Mimi, with a baby in her belly.
Saw them standing in a row
by the drystone wall, in the wind.
Saw the package move.
Saw it was stained with red and yellow.
Saw the shepherd wipe red hands on the ewe's wool.
Heard the other sheep in the meadow calling out.
Saw the package shaking its head.
Saw it try to stand. Saw it nearly succeed.
Saw it have to sit and think about it a bit.
Saw a new creature's first moments of thinking.
Felt the chill blowing through me.

Heard the shepherd say:
"Good day for lambing. Wind dries them out."
Saw the package start to stand.
Get half-way. Kneeling.
Saw it push upward. Stagger, push, and make it.
Stand. Standing.
Saw it surely was a lamb, a lamb, a lamb!
Saw a lamb being born.

DREAM AT THE DEATH OF JAMES WRIGHT

The wind is rolling the buffalo down;
the wind is shining and sharpening the buffalo
and rolling them down.
The sheep have already scattered
toward the forest,
sheep are streaming
along the stained edges of the forest.
But the wind is rolling the buffalo down.
We have not built a shelter for them,
we have put up no corral.
They don't know enough to
come together, bind their black fur
together, sit out the storm.
I see one huge one struggling
inside a lantern of grasses.
The wind is rolling the buffalo down,
shining and sharpening them
and rolling them down.

3/26/80

THINKING I HEARD A CRY AMONG THE TREES

It could have been any creature
Could have been no cry

Something I thought I heard
As I ran that dirt road early

Could have been
In these miles and miles of forest
A tree itself

Some pine a wind has moaned around
Once too often
Some aspen too rotten

It could have been
A bird whose nest's taken
Or who takes another's—
Its triumph

It could have been some creature
In a trap a man set
Or one by its own kind caught

It could have been
No cry

It could have been
Something not born for speech
The one time in time

It tries for its name
And fails

It could have been
The last of the dark's
Name for the last of the dark
Or the curse that the dark
In going
Calls to the first of the light

It could have been
Something I lack the means
To receive
Something I need to leave
The familiar for

Or it could have been
No cry
Nothing at all

No cry I heard
As I ran that early road

LEAVES ARE MY FLOWERS NOW

Leaves are my flowers now.
Basswood and sumac,
their banners and flags,
aspen and oak,
their shreds, their ribbons, their rags,
flutter and rattle.
Leaves are my flowers now.

Now is most fruit
shrunk to husk,
petal to small skull;
now are most things
gone from air,
now I see no dragonfly
out over water,
nor butterfly, with high sails
of yellow and black,
nor wasp, whom frosts
have silvered and slowed.
Now is light expert
among them, takes first
this pulse, then this one,
now shines a little
this surface, now
stains, now prescribes.

Clearer and clearer
the paths I pick.

Basswood and sumac,
their banners and flags,
aspen and oak,
their shreds, their ribbons, their rags,
flutter and rattle.
September is almost over
and leaves are my flowers now.

from ALL MY PRETTY ONES
in memory of Anne Sexton

for music by Stephen Paulus

1/ IN A TREE AT DAWN, TO LISTEN TO BIRDS

I had wanted to hide
I had wanted to stay there and hear
the whole day's songs.

I who am not satisfied
with my speech,
so heavy, so human,
I had wanted to learn their lightness,

I who am not pleased
with my name,
I had hoped they would think me
their fellow among the green
and fling me a new one.

When I had climbed back down
to where I belong,
among women, among men,
the singing began again.

3/ PURPLE FINCH

A finch with a broken neck lies by my house.
I must assume the coroner of birds would say

the neck was broken.
I suppose he flew against my window.
I take the sharp spade and dig
through the first snow. The ground
is not yet frozen, but hardening.
I dig through a thick root.
I dig past where the dogs would reach,
who are watching.
I dig through the old worlds,
where the worms still rule.
I dig past the gates and exits of that.
I dig through five kinds of color.
I dig through gold and blue and scarlet
and black and green. I dig past color.
I dig till I feel I have reached
air again, air of a quieter kind,
where he can ride,
in a time of waiting.
With a mind for all who descend
I lower the broken bird.

4/ FEEDER

The same day I build
a feeder for the winter birds,
two grosbeaks, male and female,
are feeding there.
His chest is yellow, bright,
hers milder, a kind of gray.
The feeder is fixed to a bare tree,
whose leaves these birds become,
female and male leaves,
both bright and mild.

5/ LITTLE LIFE

Life,
O little life,
what is happening to you?

You one among many,
don't you like to be
just a tree of the wood?

O little life,
let the birds come down
on you,

let them sing
above your speech,
which should diminish,

let the rains wet
you, let storms shake
you — and shine with your storm.

The earth lies deep
where your roots grip —
and your arms in air —

she guards the seeds
of space in her;
you are feeding there.

Life,
O little life,
it is happening to you.

6/ THE BIRD INSIDE

And when I am calm
the bird arrives inside.
Who slows between the eyes.
Who spreads long wings.

This is he and she of the center.
Wing Shadow. Wing Light.
And stands. And stands.
Without memory. Without desire.

Who comes when I am calm.
Who stands at the center.
Who does not feed, nor sing.
Without memory. Without desire.

Who grows. Till the skull fill,
till all my head be bird,
bird-bones be mine, and I rise.
Without memory. Without desire.

7/ NIGHT BIRD

I know what the night bird wants

choose   choose   choose   choose
   easy   easy   easy   easy

just under tongues
the night bird lives

night bird among the leaves

she has wings enough
for everyone
there is milk enough
in that breast for feeding

choose   choose   choose   choose
    easy   easy   easy   easy

she has a new name in mind
each to receive the new name
hidden just under
hidden just under
the old one

who out there, but near . . .
who nearer . . .
who nearer . . .

now   now   now   now
   in   in   in

O Mother of Bones
Mother of Names

I know what the night bird wants

8/ ALL MY PRETTY ONES

Do you see? There!
It is the grosbeak   it is the chickadee
come to crack
seeds, seeds I have set out
it is the purple finch   it is the gold

All my pretty
        all my pretty
                all my pretty ones

return

Do you hear? There!
thrum!   thrum!
wind of their wings
some singly   some paired
some with their tribe
some with a quick, a silvery
some with a slower singing

All my pretty
        all my pretty
                all my pretty ones

return

I had forgotten
I had feared to wake to songs
which ask that all of the heart be used

How many dyings
and still this singing
no question of no song
from the breast intended for singing

I had wanted to hide ...

Do you see? There!
in light now
        from shelter
                from sleep

it is the nuthatch   it is the sparrow
the thrush   the cardinal   the jay

O little life

All my pretty
            all my pretty
                        all my pretty ones
    return

YOU WON'T REMEMBER THIS
1992

MENGELE

Don't tell me about the bones of Mengele,
the bones are alive and well.
Don't think to thrill me with tales
of the drowned bones uncovered,
the bones are alive and well
inside the sleeves of a suit this day
and carving out the figures of a fat check
or severing a ribbon with the ceremonial scissors
or holding the head of a child;
I tell you, the bones are alive and well.

Don't expect me to get excited
concerning the skull of Mengele,
the skull is alive and well,
the skull is asquirm with schemes this day
and low words are leaving it at this moment
and other skulls are nodding at what they hear,
seated about the world table;
I tell you, the skull is alive and well.

Don't bother showing me pictures
of the remains of Mengele,
the remains are alive and well
and simmering in our rivers
or climbing into our houses out of the ground
where they will not be confined
or sliding inside the rain
out of the summer air, oh yes,
the remains are even there, I tell you,
are alive, are well, are everywhere.

GULF WAR DREAM

my legless son arriving home from school,
demanding to know what's on TV, which cartoons,
rings under his eyes, his seven-year-old
face pitiless: *what's on? what's on?*

first, I say, first, before TV, tell me
how you are, give me a hug, did this
happen to you in school today? tell me,
who did this to you? look at me.

he doesn't want to talk about it,
doesn't want to look, to touch, it seems
the wounds are old, it seems he gets by
quite nicely on his hands,

and pushing past me toward the TV,
white-faced, raging: *what's on? what's on?*

DRIVING SOUTH, SUNSET, FEBRUARY

House on fire, but only the glass
Fence on fire, but only the wires

Horse on fire, but only the eyes

THE HOUSE WITHOUT US

Creatures must surely come closer than now
as we sit in a circle of lawn chairs,
quiet under August stars,
some fixed, some falling.

Sometimes I'd like to be something
a little less than human,
to be able to watch
as the bear sways up
to rub his rump upon the siding,
to rub his shadow up against our absence.

Leaves, one day I'll be one of you
rather than even the most neighborly star,
nearer to those we'll have left
and all *they* love;
they too encircled under these same heavens
but in some later August of the world.

A VISIT

My parents visited me
in the form of a river;
I felt the force of that river's flood
up my spine, as though
my back were the socket to receive
my parents' double power.

I grinned like a madman in a gale.

Then my mother and father
began together to braid
the hair of my life behind me.

WEDDING FIGURES

This is not the best picture of him, she would say;
look at this one. He's more handsome here.
What is it about this one she didn't care for?
She looks utterly young, blithe, happy,
her lengthy dress has the folds of a silk statue.
Perhaps it is that he looks a little awkward,
that he is leaning a little to the left, into her,
he could be straighter, or perhaps
that the morning coat looks slightly too big for him
and the striped trousers are a bit baggy,
you can sense the pale, blue-veined legs inside,
and also that the right hand below the stiff cuff
looks rather useless, like an actor who doesn't
know what to do with his hand and lets it
hang, or is it that the wrist of the left hand,
at the end of the arm that's linked
through her right arm, looks skinny, insubstantial?
And everything of him is leaning a little
to the left, toward her, though I had never
noticed it till now, never looked closely,
and yes, the vest slopes from his right hip
at a slight angle toward his left hip, the left
shoulder is lower; why can't this man
stand straighter at the nuptial parade? And because
his head is also turned just slightly, the right ear
looks bigger, while the left is more discreet,
and the smile is even a little foolish, like
a country boy in town and over-dressed, and then
there's the small unnatural brightness where

someone has painted in the small gap between
two teeth on the right side of his mouth.

If you turn the picture over (and it is
a silhouette cut out of the original)
the white backing shows his lean absolutely
clearly pronounced, and you'd think that
someone behind them in 1936 would have
checked at the last minute, and called
straighten up, Eddie but there was no one.
The eyes, the eyes of both of them shine;
hers are larger, rounder, something more
of a serene content, but his have a boy's
gleam upon the older face, he is really joyed
to be standing here by this woman, so joyed
he can't quite keep himself still, even though
he's been posed, and he's hopping a little
from foot to foot, just slightly, not detectably,
and the shutter catches him as he's just
shifted onto the left foot, he can't quite wait
for the music to begin, and while she's standing
obedient and still before the instructions
of the picture-taker, he's started already,
and today, my dancing master, we've caught you
at your little game.

from WILD AND CALM LAMENT FOR MY MOTHER

1: Mum Before Death Dream

I saw this dream, four weeks before you died:

You stood on the pebbles of a beach.
You said: "I don't want the sea to touch me."
And then: "I am curious about the fishes
but I am not curious enough.
The earth, the twigs, the ants,
these are my friends."

In the empty sunlit town where my father
is the cobblestones, you went girl-like,
rattling a cart. You said:
"My father and mother are dead
and I am dead too. Do come
and see me some time,
stay just a little while.

"I am safe in the sunlight in the empty town."

2: Late Bird

Why is it the late bird who draws me now,
where once it was the early?

O early bird, I wrote and wrote of you
till perhaps it was tiresome.
But now the late bird sings and sings,
so heedlessly, into the arms of dark.

Night is no weight for her; she is freed,
I think, by the dark, or pours

more purely for knowing it is she alone
who continues, unseen.

I read, I write. Even when I turn off my lamp
and roll toward sleep,

she is still at her song.

3: The Night You Died

The night you died I dreamed
a banal sexual dream, which,
when I woke, reminded me
of my old faithless life.

Things you never knew I did,
trees standing in water.

In that same dark a bird beat
again and again at the window,
so that at first light we strung
red rags against the glass.

Huge, these robins.
Strange how, after all these years,
still I expect them
to be little, the English kind.

4: The Trees

All across the air I saw
the trees you sent, the forests
of England uprooted, hurled horizontal;
you had now no tender thoughts
for the nests and younglings,
you tore up the trees
and sent them. I saw them pass.

Not the doodle-bugs the Jerries sent
while we shivered under the stairs,
but the huge exposed
root systems of English
beeches and oaks, the stained
muddy turbines hurtling by,
Epping, Sherwood, the Forest of Dean,
the Atlantic just a ditch at your death
and they leapt it.

Sent me your seas too, roused, whirling,
chopped by the cleavers of winds,
sent me your low scurrying clouds,
a rushing of gangs and packs,
a trailing of torn bellies,
giblet gangs, gizzard gangs,

sent me your dissolving,
beamed out your dissolution
upon me, the one devoutly
wished for but feared and suddenly
here, here, the body

scarcely prepared as the spirit
adieus it,

sent me against all winds your weathers,
so that I guttered,
your rains so that I streamed,
poured out your mourning grains,
the barns at last broken open, spilling
the stored years,

sent your sad hours on me,
beamed me your grieving,
so that my hair grew long
in a day, so that I stopped
to weep on the doorsteps,
your features, so that for days
I went about widowed, bearded,
with your face.

5: *The Alleys*

Running the alleys. St Paul. Mid-June.
You're four days dead. No one
will know I am mourning you.
I love these concrete lanes,
these stained neglected zones where nothing's
discouraged, where weeds, where flies
can get an education, where whatever
is crammed beneath lids is urged
to bulge its own way out, where
leaves and vines mutter, multiplying,
where chained dogs moan or flaunt

their fangs or whine and piss
at the pleasure of somebody passing.

It is not stable, this weather.
Above, the frontier sky-towns,
not stable. Bruised light. An electric
thriving over us. Last night,
one storm, another, everything
shaking, streaming, shining.
Collapse of those towns, rubbling us.
And I run to the rhythms
of last night's storms, to the rhythms
of those to come.

At the little flat,
peaceful, in your nightgown,
your hand on your breast.
They broke in.

No one will know I am mourning you.
Not able to be there,
I run, to blame for these storms.

"She'd be mad if you came," said Angela.
"Besides, she's international now."

I remember your narrow home
in London, where the four sisters,
Winifred and Nora and Julie and Molly,
grew up learning to talk "nicely,"
and that you passed on to me —

"Not jography, darling, *geography*."
And your prizes for elocution, for Shakespeare;
always you relished, always could retrieve —

I know a bank where the wild thyme blows,
Where oxlips and the nodding violet grows.

Sometimes I wonder where
my own voice belongs, on what
street, on what ground.

I remember the trip up to London
when Granny died, going for you
because of your operation, remember
Grandpa weeping and Granny laid out,
so little, so lined, her long gray hair
coiled as always behind her head,
and that low attentive Irish voice
gone forever from the chilled head
I bent to kiss.

No one will know I am mourning you.
Not able to kiss, I run
these New World lanes, between storms,

> *Over hill, over dale,*

past pails overflowing with outtakes
of lilacs,

> *Thorough bush, thorough brier,*

split baby shoes, ripped
cereal boxes,

> *Over park, over pale,*
> *Thorough flood, thorough fire,*

dull brown and green
of wine bottles,

> *I do wander everywhere,*
> *Swifter than the moon's sphere,*

and all over
the crushed, upended cartons of milk,
drained by the hungry mouths and discarded.

> *And I serve the Fairy Queen,*
> *To dew her orbs upon the green.*

8: I Should Bloody Well Hope So

You fell down; later, you wouldn't admit
you had fallen. Once you said:
"I always escape in my dreams."
Driving around England in the rented car:
churches, picnics, nice little pubs.
"I can't believe this is happening to me.
I feel as if I'm living
in some strange sort of dream."

Once you wrote poems. You said:
"I'm just going to sit down and let my words
come out the way they want to."

On the phone:
"I love you too much, you'll never know."
"I love you to bits."

Of modern art:
"Picasso used to paint such lovely things,
but then he went all strange, poor darling."

At home: "I always see faces ... in the fir tree
always, always I see a face.
When I sit outside, I see faces
in the clouds.
My chair is right opposite the clouds."

In the last weeks: "How strange life is.
It goes all the way down
to the beetle, everything
feeds on everything".

"Sun ... wind ... trees . . . birds.
When your flesh rots away from your bones,
where do you go?"

"I love you, Mum."
I should bloody well hope so."

11: All Over. Fear No More.

All over, the little flat,
where you felt safe, more or less,
days with the telly on,
to have people there,

the apple slices and barley water
on the table by your chair.

All over, the walls of faces,
the children, grandchildren, nieces, nephews,
the Sacred Heart, Our Lady of Lourdes,
Father Bertrand, whose death seemed to scare you,
Uncle Frank, whose death shook you,
Daddy, whose death uprooted you.

All over, the diminished life,
the clouds drifting or rolling
over the Surrey hills, the blazered
children chattering to school
and back from school,
the milkman, the postman, the knock
on the double-locked door ("Who is it?").
Fear no more
        the trip to the store,
Fear no more
        the afternoons, the years,
Fear no more
        the struggling up from the chair,
        the trying to get to the phone,
Fear no more
        the waking alone with pain,
        the dishes piled, the spiders
        sprinkling their blue silences
        about you.

        Old origin,
Fear no lonely more.

*12: I'm Sorry to Hear Your Mother is Dead. How Are
You Feeling?*

Inside the body
many miles of canals, minor rivers,
windings of weedy backwaters.
A punt sliding by, a slow skiff,
an angler dozing.

Plenty of quiet little pubs
in that land, where my parents
can sip their pints.
The children? They're around somewhere,
they're near, you can hear
their cries. They're happy.

I carry old churches inside me,
sweet air of incense from mass,
the kissing and lighting of candles,
swift whispered prayers, then out
into sun, or drizzle, or wind.
I carry that mother and father inside me,
I'm a hall of syllables
where their low voices are murmuring
secrets I've not forgotten.

In the tape of the service you can hear
the old hymns she wanted and got,
thanks a lot, Mum, not a dry eye
there, then, in the old world,
nor here now, in the new,
you can hear the voice of the celebrant,

Father Kemble, my old Chemistry teacher,
intoning over "the body of this our sister,
which we are about to bury,"
leading the farewell to
"our sister Winifred," you can hear
behind him the sounds of traffic
along Heath Road, Weybridge, where
the polished cars will soon creep,
left at the bottom of the hill,
right in a few hundred yards onto
the gravelled drive of the cemetery,

you can hear "may the angels bring you
into the arms of Abraham ...
till we all meet in Christ ..." and the final
dogged playing of Brahms' St. Anthony Chorale
which Daddy would have died to hear,
his organ, after all, *his* instrument,
and then the end of the tape, the hiss
and crackle of nothing left to record,
you can sit and listen to that if you want,
because who's to stop you?

Old loves, what do I say
but that daily I go back
to what you gave, say
it is given still, out of
an endless wellspring,
that wherever I travel
it is proper to talk to you,
as I do and will?

Whatever street I am on, the feeling
that somewhere you *are.*

These lambs about me, their leaping,
the wife I am learning continually
to love, if I cannot
name these amazements daily,
how am I your son? The days
ease into another summer,
old branches recover their green,
and these faces, in whom I see you,
lean, oh, eagerly, toward the world.
What I ask, old loves, of you,
is the courage, the praise
the difficult world deserves,
as we go on into whatever
our lives will become,
into its singing, which in us

you began.

TO SHOW PETER THE WORLD

Are we, perhaps, here just for saying:
house, bridge, well, gate, jug, fruit-tree, window . . .

— R. M. Rilke (Ninth Duino Elegy)

It seems as if sometimes in sleep
the names drift off from their things.
The name-mist lifts. The things shine, clean.
On other nights the usual heavens
slide under and are gone.
New constellations gleam, suggestive.

It seems that I am bound to be
yet one more Adam, with my seven-month son;
not Lear, exhausted, bearing his daughter
at the very end of things, vowing
with all music what can never be, but
at the beginning, Peter, in truth
at the start of it all. *We two will sing.*

There are days, child, I have woken
ashamed of the names, wanting,
for your entering, fresher ones
for what you will come to know,
and what I must learn to do, all
over again, is trust the necessity,
the endlessness, the grace of our naming,
which is human, which is what we do,
and sound again around lips and teeth and tongue,
and roll again down bones and veins,
familiar syllables, yes, the usual ones,

until they assume the unknown again,
until no name's familiar, and learn

not only to wander with you
the present borders of our naming
but to be there to watch and listen
as you begin going on beyond,
making *your* names for the things, as
Peter shows Peter the world, this place
into which we have only brought you,
and in which we must leave you.

PETER AND THUNDER

Your face when you heard it. How you looked up.
How, crouched over toy parts,
suddenly you stiffened. How then you turned,
how you stared up in the direction
of the thunder. *They are at the gates.*
How then you looked at me, as if
I might send them away, as if with a few
low-toned, well-chosen words I could
send the thunder-gangs scuttling back
through all the holes in the sky.
As if there were no thunder deep
down in my own bones, no thunder
in yours, little son.

DANCING FOR HIM

He likes to watch us dance, we do it
for him, he laughs, we waltz
around him in the kitchen or polka,
leaping, through the living room, he
laughs, or cheek to cheek like
a dragged-out marathon couple we
slouch and stagger, he throws back
his months' old head and laughs.

What he'll remember of these times,
who knows? Maybe one morning,
waking from a dream of faces,
he'll turn to one beside him, saying:
"That's it! They used to dance for me!"

YOU WON'T REMEMBER THIS
for Peter and Mary and Nellie

1

You lift your arms to your head,
which looks so dark, then turn
to lie on your side, the fluid
swilling in your abdomen.
The radiologist says:

"Anything dark is liquid,
anything white is muscle,
anything gray is bone."

These like the moon pictures,
wavering, grainy, the lens
lurching, and again you turn;
that shadowy bulb is your head,
those snow streaks your muscles,
those blurred tundras your bones.

you won't remember this

At ten days
you look lonely.
You seem between countries.

You look at me briefly,
not with interest.
You give no sign.

I toss you shreds of song
to where you lie,
down in the cradle canyon,
looking up.

Remote to you my moon
drifts over the rim.

You lie,
looking up.

> *you won't remember this*

Today your first injection,
and tonight you cry, your thigh
throbbing. Now you have fallen
asleep on my left shoulder,
lying across my heart.

> *you won't remember this*

You don't want to go
to day care today; you weep,
you cling to my leg,
you roll your eyes:
oh no oh no; all the sorrows
of my mother in my daughter.

> *you won't remember this*

I hear a moaning from upstairs;
slowly you descend — *whooo whooo whooo* —

over your head the nibbled blanket;
on the last tread trip, topple
— *oops! oops!* —
and I gather up my ghost.

you won't remember this

Yesterday you set up a stall on a table,
invited us to buy. "How much is *this?*" we asked.
"About ten hundred," you said, frowning
at a pair of plastic feet.

Daily you bring us gifts with a shy face,
and watch us while we open them —
say a box with a wooden lid and in it
your yellow hairbrush, scraps of paper or card
with your green and blue coloring on them —
they're maps, you say, of the ocean, the sky.
Sometimes pictures we've cut out for you
that now you give back, wide-eyed
at our delight at getting them from you.
Daily you assemble such treasures and appear.

you won't remember this

2

Cresting the stony hill, the edge of England,
        and there was the sea,
the holiday town our parents brought us to
        when I was fourteen.
I found the dunes where we'd tumbled,

swam in those waves again,
the breakers forever rolling in
from the new world.

Such a boy I was then, all aware
of myself in the waves;
but now the salted element itself
and look, so many the swimmers.

At the country pub, sitting
on the same stone wall,
but now with Peter, six, and still
the leafy pulse of wood doves —
Hoo HOO Hoo, Hoo HOO Hoo —
I wonder how I could want them back,
who are done with the human.
Let them go.
Hoo HOO Hoo. Hoo HOO Hoo.

Heading home, we'd drive the moth-thick dark,
wind-burned and dreamy,
both of them leading us in songs,
easeful baritone, meticulous soprano,
and we'd chorus on,
the waves, the doves, the gulls, the hedgerows
flashing inside us
as we slid toward sleep.

And here my mother's little notebook now,
its English addresses and numbers,
her late night wartime notes to my father,
(at last we're sleeping),

some of my father's letters to her,
          some to *his* father:
"As I walk the streets of the City — your city —
          when I hear old tunes, oh!
in so many other ways
          which my poor pen cannot describe,
I think of you constantly.

Love beyond naming, what will we keep
when we've let go of all remembering,
what can we know when we've relinquished
all rooms, all limbs, all breathing?
Gardens of daughters and sons we've tended
and must leave, remember?
Lips and foreheads we will still want to kiss
when we've no mouths for kissing,
remember?

3

Night. Night light. Now you are sleeping,
far from our own childhoods, deep in yours.
Nothing, loves, to remember,
no day, no street, no sky,
only rooms scribbled on water,
voices chasing voices
down corridors of seas, all the old
cargoes rolling. Unless we become
as you, we won't enter.

In such a sleep as this, when all day
is forgotten and runs like a river

under the skull, dividing
and tumbling up a million tributaries,
when the air is all words and leaves,
the garages adrift, the old barns wandering,
and even the careful stones are unstrung,
then, mother, then, father,
go into the dream with them,
where the grief we are separate
is not known, till even
Abraham is understood, who would have
let go his son.

As you laugh, children, as you cry
out in your sleep, as you are blind,
as you are ghosts to the day
(though I love the days)
as the tongue has nothing to tell,
slumped like a beast on straw,
as the wine of the crushed days
spills and the ripe clocks burst,
releasing their seeds to the air,
then like climbers roped by the silks
of sleep, fragrant with the dreams
and forgetting of those mists,
we wander together.

Unless we become as you, we won't enter,
who have forgotten what the world will be,
to swim with you that dark unmaking
where the new life forms.

4

Someone should tell the dreamer to rise.
A day's begun that needs you; stir the fire.
Sleepers for sure, and soon, will need you,
swaying or stumbling down the stairs.
Hoo HOO Hoo. Hoo HOO Hoo.
Liquid, muscle, bone. Hold them.
Go with them into the day.

EVENSONG

"There he is" he learns to say
when we glimpse the great sun burning down
toward the hill, and "There she is"
when we spot the pale enormous moon
floating low above the pines;
and over and over, swiveling his head,
he says it as I drive them both,
daughter and son, around the roads
until they sleep, so I can have
dinner and an hour alone with their mother.

Ahead in the shadows, two deer.
A little further, metal abandoned
in somebody's yard, auto parts
and ancient appliances, that later
the moon will make into something,
that same skilled stranger keeping us
company beyond the branches.

He wants to know why they share the sky,
and all I can tell him is it's a secret
we have to guess at as we go;
and "There he is" he says once more
as the hill prepares to swallow fire,
and "There she is" as she climbs the air,
and murmurs and murmurs until he sleeps
(and she already is sleeping).

NEW POEMS

ON THE ANNIVERSARY

The only doors that I know
for you to come through are within,
and there you have appeared
from time to time,
may appear again.

Old son that I am,
I welcome my wandering father
when he wills —
let him come, let him go
any hour, arriving
with no warning, leaving
with no assurances.

Saying goodnight last night
to my boy, I could hear you;
carrying my dreaming girl
to her proper bed, I remembered
your own pale body
our final summer,
the veins blue as rivers
as you led us to water.

Wherever the son
may travel, let there be
doors without number
where the father may enter.

ADVENT LIMBO

We do an early walk, the dog and I.
Easy for him, for me. I love
bare branches, the wild cold air.
Together we're fine. And you?
You put your right leg on mine,
show me the veins, tell me you feel
in pain all the time. Yesterday,
your stroll by the river, I hoped
you'd come home better, but
"My stomach muscles are so tight,
I had trouble walking."

Yesterday brought you a rose,
hoping its petals
might remind the veins, heal
fears for the labor, for the health
of the hidden child,
wishing I could bring back
your brother's first-born son,
little solstice,
who lived two hours,

or the children
open the calendar to find
a day without veins,
the landscape of a body
you can accept, an ease
as of water, where you feel
no less floating than the one
within you. You stroke your belly

round and round, together we sing
toward the one now soon to come
into this daily living, dying that we do.
Help us keep learning how to wait,
this advent of our final child,
as gusts unhinge the icy branches,
as dark whirls down,
and street after frozen street,
however wind or dark can moan or warn,
the lights come on.

FOR A BIRTH
for John McLean

My heart has been light all day
at the thought of the boy
who only last night burst from the dark
into arms that had ached for him,
who only three days past the feast
of those wandering, worshipping kings
unfolded himself, full gift and mystery
from the depths of our laboring life.

If you have flung the wreath from your door,
restore it now,
or run to gather fresh green from the trees of life,
for that which was lost is found,
the cold month shines
with the harvest we hardly could hope for,
and his being blazes from the hill-top
of every heart which will come to love him.

I BELIEVE ANITA HILL

Darkness is falling

That microphone clipped
To his lapel

Could be a twig or a stick beetle
Or even a snail.

Were this not a senate hearing
But the forest floor

Something is crawling

THE NOW, THE LONG AGO

In the dream time of the swarming snow
We're on the couch, just chatting, you and I,
Here in the now, there in the long ago.

The world outside is singular and slow,
As if the winter taught all things to sigh
In the dream time of the swarming snow.

I'll make our supper, then we'll watch a show,
And then you'll choose some stories, by and by,
Here in the now, there in the long ago.

So many things that you don't need to know
About the years, the years that simplify
In the dream time of the swarming snow.

This won't go on forever, child, although
I've never had the words to tell you why,
Here in the now, there in the long ago,

Won't be for always, little love, and so
We'll take this all as blessing, you and I,
In the dream time of the swarming snow,
Here in the now, there in the long ago.

THREE FAWNS

Surely they will not go with us
          into the other life,
these three among the ferns?
          We will not take them,
they'll make it on their own,
          wounded or slain,
into some radiance of slender pine
          much like the one
I saw them in this morning
          on my early run.
And maybe whole parts of this earth
          (I pray - the rivers)
will be there with us
          whatever the form, unform
we'll wear in that life,
          the one those startled faces
set me to dreaming of,
          and dreaming then of my children,
their widened eyes,
          (and thoughts of them
always lead me to paradise).

CARNEGIE MELLON POETRY

1981
A Little Faith, John Skoyles
Augers, Paula Rankin
Walking Home from the Icehouse, Vern Rutsala
Work and Love, Stephen Dunn
The Rote Walker, Mark Jarman
Morocco Journal, Richard Harteis
Songs of a Returning Soul, Elizabeth Libbey

1982
The Granary, Kim R. Stafford
Calling the Dead, C.G. Hanzlicek
Dreams Before Sleep, T. Alan Broughton
Sorting It Out, Anne S. Perlman
Love Is Not a Consolation; It Is a Light, Primus St. John

1983
The Going Under of the Evening Land, Mekeel McBride
Museum, Rita Dove
Air and Salt, Eve Shelnutt
Nightseasons, Peter Cooley

1984
Falling from Stardom, Jonathan Holden
Miracle Mile, Ed Ochester
Girlfriends and Wives, Robert Wallace
Earthly Purposes, Jay Meek
Not Dancing, Stephen Dunn
The Man in the Middle, Gregory Djanikian
A Heart Out of This World, David James
All You Have in Common, Dara Wier

1985
Smoke from the Fires, Michael Dennis Browne
Full of Lust and Good Usage, Stephen Dunn (2nd edition)
Far and Away, Mark Jarman
Anniversary of the Air, Michael Waters
To the House Ghost, Paula Rankin
Midwinter Transport, Anne Bromley

1986
Seals in the Inner Harbor, Brendan Galvin
Thomas and Beulah, Rita Dove
Further Adventures With You, C.D. Wright
Fifteen to Infinity, Ruth Fainlight
False Statements, Jim Hall
When There Are No Secrets, C.G. Hanzlicek

1987
Some Gangster Pain, Gillian Conoley
Other Children, Lawrence Raab
Internal Geography, Richard Harteis
The Van Gogh Notebook, Peter Cooley
A Circus of Needs, Stephen Dunn (2nd edition)
Ruined Cities, Vern Rutsala
Places and Stories, Kim R. Stafford

1988
Preparing to Be Happy, T. Alan Broughton
Red Letter Days, Mekeel McBride
The Abandoned Country, Thomas Rabbitt
The Book of Knowledge, Dara Wier
Changing the Name to Ochester, Ed Ochester
Weaving the Sheets, Judith Root

1989
Recital in a Private Home, Eve Shelnutt
A Walled Garden, Michael Cuddihy
The Age of Krypton, Carol J. Pierman
Land That Wasn't Ours, David Keller
Stations, Jay Meek
The Common Summer: New and Selected Poems, Robert Wallace
The Burden Lifters, Michael Waters
Falling Deeply into America, Gregory Djanikian
Entry in an Unknown Hand, Franz Wright

1990
Why the River Disappears, Marcia Southwick
Staying Up For Love, Leslie Adrienne Miller
Dreamer, Primus St. John

1991

Permanent Change, John Skoyles
Clackamas, Gary Gildner
Tall Stranger, Gillian Conoley
The Gathering of My Name, Cornelius Eady
A Dog in the Lifeboat, Joyce Peseroff
Raised Underground, Renate Wood
Divorce: A Romance, Paula Rankin

1992

Modern Ocean, James Harms
The Astonished Hours, Peter Cooley
You Won't Remember This, Michael Dennis Browne
Twenty Colors, Elizabeth Kirschner
First A Long Hesitation, Eve Shelnutt
Bountiful, Michael Waters
Blue for the Plough, Dara Wier
All That Heat in a Cold Sky, Elizabeth Libbey

1993

Trumpeter, Jeannine Savard
Cuba, Ricardo Pau-Llosa
The Night World and the Word Night, Franz Wright
The Book of Complaints, Richard Katrovas

1994

If Winter Come: Collected Poems, 1967–1992, Alvin Aubert
Of Desire and Disorder, Wayne Dodd
Ungodliness, Leslie Adrienne Miller
Rain, Henry Carlile
Windows, Jay Meek
A Handful of Bees, Dzvinia Orlowsky

1995

Germany, Caroline Finkelstein
Housekeeping in a Dream, Laura Kasischke
About Distance, Gregory Djanikian
Wind of the White Dresses, Mekeel McBride
Above the Tree Line, Kathy Mangan

In the Country of Elegies, T. Alan Broughton
Scenes from the Light Years, Anne C. Bromley
Quartet, Angela Ball
Rorschach Test, Franz Wright

1996
Back Roads, Patricia Henley
Dyer's Thistle, Peter Balakian
Beckon, Gillian Conoley
The Parable of Fire, James Reiss
Cold Pluto, Mary Ruefle
Orders of Affection, Arthur Smith
Colander, Michael McFee

1997
Growing Darkness, Growing Light, Jean Valentine
Selected Poems, 1965-1995, Michael Dennis Browne
Your Rightful Childhood: New and Selected Poems, Paula Rankin
Headlands: New and Selected Poems, Jay Meek
Soul Train, Allison Joseph
The Autobiography of a Jukebox, Cornelius Eady
The Patience of the Cloud Photographer, Elizabeth Holmes
Madly in Love, Aliki Barnstone